SILLY
WARNING!
Do
not
read
this
book
while
you
are
standing
up
because
it
could
make
you
laugh
so
hard
you
might
fall
down
and
break
your
crown.

Beautifully spoken,
Boodleheimer. I
couldn't have said
it better myself.

To Joe
who was "J.B.," age five, when he inspired me
to create *The Silly Book* . . .

To Henry
who was one-year-old "Hanky" way back in 1961 . . .

To Martha
who wasn't even born yet . . .

And to Zack
who didn't check in for another 16 years

S.H.

P.S. And to Jamie Michalak and the Lovely Ann Stott, whose
passion for the book make Ursula Nordstrom live again.

First Candlewick Press edition 2004

Library of Congress Cataloging-in-Publication Data is available.

Library of Congress Catalog Card Number 2003051603

ISBN 0-7636-2256-7

2 4 6 8 10 9 7 5 3 1

Printed in China

This book was typeset in Handwriter and hand lettered by the illustrator.
The illustrations were done in ink and digitally colorized.

Candlewick Press
2067 Massachusetts Avenue
Cambridge, Massachusetts 02140

visit us at www.candlewick.com

the Silly Book

Stoo Hample

CANDLEWICK PRESS
CAMBRIDGE, MASSACHUSETTS

SILLY SONG

(Make up your own silly tune.)

Boodleheimer
Boodleheimer

(CLAP! CLAP! CLAP!)

Boodleheimer
Boodleheimer

(CLAP! CLAP! CLAP!)

The more you Boodle,
The less you Heimer.
The more you Heimer,
The less you Boodle.

Boodleheimer
Boodleheimer

(CLAP! CLAP! CLAP!)

Now
you
have
to
sing
it
again
or
else
you
will
turn
into
a
bathtub!

SILLY THINGS TO SAY

(to a leopard)

Mr. Leopard,
Please pass the
Salt and peppard.

(to an alligator)

Hello, alligator.
Would you like to be
My palligator?

(when you have a cold)

I feel awful
When I sneeze and cawful.

(to the dentist)

Be nice to my teeth
Pleeth!

(to the gas station man)

Something's the mattery
With my battery.

GRRR!

(to a growly tiger)

I don't like you
Even a *little*
Bittle!

ANOTHER SILLY SONG

(So you have to make up another silly tune.)

My daddy flew me to the moon,
moon,
moon.
My daddy flew me to the moon.
And when we got there, what did we see?
But a great big fuzzy Moon Goon,
Moon Goon.
A great big fuzzy Moon Goon.

ANOTHER, ANOTHER SILLY SONG

(So you have to make up *another*, another silly tune.)

Gong!
Gong!
Gong!
This is a silly song.
A silly silly silly silly silly silly song.
Gong!
Gong!
Gong!

Bong!
Bong!
Bong!
A silly silly silly silly songity songity song.
Gong!
Bong!
Gong!

Bong!
Gong!
Beep!
(Oops!)
Bong!

I'M
BOODLEHEIMER.

I'M
MOTHER
GOOSE.

SILLY NAMES

(To call people and things)

Call Daddy: "Mommy"

Call Mommy: "Daddy"

Call Brother: "Nobody"

Call Sister: "Potato"

Call Doggie: "Horse Face"

Call Milk: "Peanut Butter"

Call Birdie: "Teddy Bear"

Call Boodleheimer: "Heimerboodle"

SILLY LILY

I am silly,
You are silly,
All of us are silly,
Willy.
All of us but cousin Millie.
She's the willy-nilly dilly
With a lily she calls "Tillie."
I think "Tillie"
Is a silly
Name for her to call a lily.
So I went and got a lily.
And I call *my* lily . . .
"Max."

SILLY STORY

I want to see my mommy a minute,
My mimmy a monnit,
My mommy a minnit.
I want to see my monny a mimmit
To sing her a little song.

To sing her a little,
To ling her a sittle,
To sit her a lingle long.

(I think my mommy will like it
Because it's a very short long.)

ANOTHER SILLY STORY

Once upon a time
In a big white house
That was red all over
(Except the roof,
Which was black)
There lived a Very Very Very Very
Old Lady
(Who was five-and-a-half years old)
And her faithful duck,
Chicken Face.
One bright
Sunny day
The old lady looked outside
And said to the duck,
"Oh dear, Chicken Face,
It is raining!
What do you think of that?"

And Chicken Face said,
"Bow-wow!"

BOW-WOW!

THAT'S ALL! GOOD BYE! TURN THE PAGE!

SILLY STUFF WITH NUMBERS

It's not much fun
To be a ONE.
But I'd rather be a one
Than *none*!

I can count to
TWO.
Can you
Count to
Two,
Too?

Me?
I can count to THREE!

When it's FOUR o'clock
It's more o'clock
Than three o'clock.

A FIVE diving a dive.

SIX
Chicks . . .

Standing on
Sticks . . .

Balanced on
Bricks.

Two SEVENs lying down
Make ears for Boodleheimer.

I just ate
An EIGHT.
And I feel great.

I just ate a NINE.
And I feel fine.

I will eat a TEN!
What will you do then?

(I'M STUFFED!)

I will eat
10, 9, 8, 7, 6,
5, 4, 3, 2, 1
With jelly—on a bun!

SILLY PERSON

I once saw a man who was so big
He looked to me just like a pig.
But he wasn't a pig—I could tell
   by his feet.
And I knew I was right when he said,
   "Tweet, tweet."

SILLY POEM

H-O-T spells "cold."
D-O-G spells "cat."
2 and 2 are 5.
Now what do you think of that?

SILLY QUESTION

If people get chicken pox,
What do chickens get?

SILLY ANSWER
People pox.

ANOTHER SILLY QUESTION

If Mommy eats a Popsicle,
What does Daddy eat?

ANOTHER SILLY ANSWER
A Momsicle!

SILLY LONDON BRIDGE

London Bridge is falling up,
falling up, falling up,
London Bridge is falling up,
My fair pickle.

SILLY SECRET

(SHHH!)

This is the silliest secret
You ever heard!
When you find out what it is
You will laugh like anything.
(Ha ha ha ha ha ha ha!)

Boy, it sure is silly!
When you hear what it is
You will giggle like a gigglecopter.
*(Giggle giggle giggle giggle!
Copter copter copter copter!)*

I think it must be
The silliest secret in the whole world.
It is so silly
It will make you roll on the floor.
(Roll roll roll roll roll.)

Would you like to know
What the silly secret is?
Well, I can't tell you.
(Sob sob sob sob sob sob!)

I forgot it!

SILLY STUFF ABOUT FURNITURE

Where is the
chair?

Over there
combing his hair.

Do you like
this couch?

No!
He's a grouch!

SILLY BACKWARDS TALK

The things I like to eat best for fastbreak
are juice orange, mealoat, and cakepans.

SILLY CLOTHES

A turtle-neck sweater
for a giraffe.

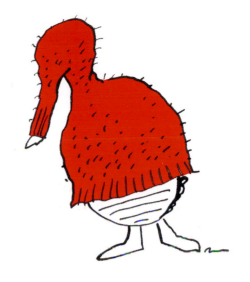

A giraffe-neck sweater
for a turtle.

SILLY MILLIE

I am silly,
You are silly,
All of us are silly,
Willy.
All of us but cousin
Millie.
She's upside down.

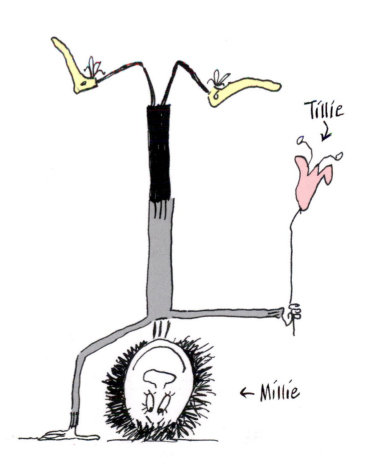

Tillie

← Millie

SILLY RECIPE

Cook three pieces of
spaghetti in a pan of
water for two years.

 Add one teaspoonful
of chocolate syrup
and mix well.

Spread on bread
and freeze.

Feed to teddy bear.

UGH!

A
SILLY
THING
TO
EAT
IS
A
CHOCOLATE
MILK
SANDWICH.

A SILLY PLEASE

A SILLY THANK YOU

A SILLY YOU'RE WELCOME

SILLY NOTHINGS

(How many can you find?)

Ha, ha. This is
not a silly nothing.
It's a silly <u>something</u>!

SILLY NURSERY RHYMES

SILLY LITTLE MISS MUFFET

Little Miss Muffet
Sat on a tuffet
Eating a pizza named Fred.
Along came a spider
Who doused it with cider,
So she plopped it right over his head.

SILLY HUMPTY DUMPTY

Humpty Dumpty sat on a wall.
Humpty Dumpty had a great fall.
All the king's horses
And all the king's men
Had scrambled eggs.

SILLY GOOD-NIGHT SONG

(Show this to Mommy and Daddy and tell them what they have to sing.)

YOU SING:

"Good Mommy, night."

"Good Daddy, night."

MOMMY SINGS:

"Now be sure to brush your bed."

DADDY SINGS:

"And go right to teeth."

ANOTHER SILLY GOOD-NIGHT SONG

(If you can't think of another silly melody, try "Mary Had a Little Lamb.")

Eat your bread and butterfly,
Butterfly,
Butterfly.
Eat your bread and butterfly,
And then go right to teeth!

HERE'S HOW TO
MAKE THE SILLY
GOOD-NIGHT SONGS
EVEN SILLIER...

SING THEM IN THE
MORNING WHEN
YOU GET UP!

WAIT! BEFORE YOU CLOSE THIS BOOK! You have to remember to remember: nothing in it is real. All of it is SILLY!
No, it's not! It's SALLY!
WRONG! I'M Sally! So ha, ha to YOU, Bunny Head!